TAMERTON FOLIOT

Arthur L. Clamp

The railway station with the stationmaster and his wife, Mr. and Mrs. Hancock, with Bert Lamble as the porter.

This version of the book is virtually as originally published.
There are now additional pages at the back providing information about the author.

The republishing project is being managed by Arthur's grandson, Steven Gibson. We aim to find all the research that he was involved in publishing, preserving it for the next generation as part of 'The Clamp Collection'.

INTRODUCTION

THIS ILLUSTRATED booklet on Tamerton Foliot should not be taken as a "history" of the village; its purpose is rather to show as many aspects as possible of people, places and events from the past eighty years as seen through the eyes of local people taking photographs of one another not anticipating that one day they may appear in a book! This coverage of the village life during these years is far from complete, many buildings have gone, patterns of everyday life are changing and events of yesteryear are, in most cases, now pleasant memories in the minds of local senior citizens. The object of this publication is simply to make a permanent record of some of the comings and goings of Tamerton, not to record all the facts and trace its developments a task which must be left to more knowledgeable persons.

Tamerton was incorporated into Plymouth in 1951 yet of all the localities surrounding the city which now form part of its large area it can rightly claim to have retained its village appearance and atmosphere more than any other place. Indeed when walking along the roads or down the creek one could quite easily conclude that the valley was miles from any main area of population. It is about five miles north of the city centre, it has access to the sea past Warleigh Point and down the Tamar, it possesses a very fine church, had a railway station, manor house, three public houses and can still boast of the "Tamerton Strawberry Fair", a well known annual event throughout the area.

Its people have left their mark on the locality in the form of buildings, both secular and religious, farms, large private residences, slaughterhouse, old wharves, horticultural enterprises, blacksmith, small industrial buildings such as the mill, shops, roads and bridges and many other small things in the way of milestones, a village pump, ornamental ironwork, etc.

It was predominantly a self sufficient community where the need to "go to town" was perhaps once a month at the most. Independence was the key of yesterdays' citizens. Clothes were hand made, much of the family food was grown in the home garden or allotment and the local farms would readily supply milk, cream, butter, etc., and meat when animals were slaughtered. Its children had the opportunities of as good an education as other villages through the endowed Mary Dean's School, entertainment of a wide variety was available through the enthusiasm of many people by staging plays, festivities and other similar events in the parish "hut". Other events on the village calendar were the char-a-banc outings when people travelled together and not singly as most do today in the car, local football matches, visitors coming up by boats and a host of minor activities which brought people together.

People still come together of course, and for many reasons, a new one being the protection of their village from over development through the watchful eye of the conservation society set up in 1975. The area has seen the steady outward growth of housing estates from the city and also from Southway. Some farms have gone, fields built upon and the rural patterns of a few years ago have almost disappeared. These are now times of caring for the environment when the pleasures and pastimes of yesterday have taken on a new meaning. *Tamerton Foliot, Portrait of a Village and Its People,* is just one attempt at focusing attention on a few decades that have passed almost too quickly in the wake of modern developments, fast means travel and the now ever present screen of television.

In gathering together these pictures and preparing the accompanying text I am greatly indebted to many people still living in the village and others who are now resident away from the area.

My first expression of thanks must go to Miss Betty Bryant through whose boundless enthusiasm for getting this collection together and therefore making this publication possible must not go unrecorded. A well known member of a family that have lived in the village for hundreds of years she is, perhaps, the most competent to judge the value of such a record as this book, in spite of its shortcomings. Many people have made useful suggestions, prodded memories and loaned photographs. Among these are Mrs. E. Mills, Mrs. B. Carter, Mrs. V. Bryant, Mrs. N. Reddicliffe, Mrs. I Tilbury, Mrs. M. Pilgrim, Mrs. J. Tooze, Mrs. F. Brimacombe, Mrs. D. Short, Mr. J. Floyd, Mrs. D. Finnemore, Mrs. P. Warne, Mrs. E. Sobey, Mr. P. Bebbington, Mrs. D. Mashford, and Mrs. L. Richards. The *Western Morning News* kindly gave permission for the large cover photograph to be included.

During the night of Friday, 18th September, 1981, fire broke out in the roof of the parish church of St. Mary's causing considerable damage to the structure and fabric of this very fine building. As the sale of this book is taking place a few weeks after this unfortunate occurence part of its sale will be donated to the restoration fund.

Arthur L. Clamp,
October, 1981.

School Football Team

Some of the young people of the village are seen in 1946 proudly assembled for the photographer, Gilbert Crotty, Ivor Paul, P. Smith, Roland Morgan, Brian Solomon, Edward May, Gordon Smith, George Hoskin, Robin Finnemore and Tony Smith form the group.

Tamerton Drama Group

These performers are outside the British Legion Hall, Crownhill; the year is 1925. Among them are M. Blackler, R. Stevens, F. Chanter, L. Richards, Mrs. Harvey, P. Maker, Mrs. G. Stephenson, P. Baron, M. Baron, K. Newcombe and K. Langman. They were members of the Tamerton Drama and Operatic Society.

1950 Drama Group Presentation

The old Parish Hall was used for many purposes including the presentation of plays, dramas, and light entertainments. This scene comes from a drama play staged in 1950. Some of the actors have been recognised. These are W. Baker, E. Sobey, W. Condon and Mrs. W. Worth.

Looking up Fore Street

Changed slightly but still recognisable this lower part of Fore Street was where Leonard Pilgrim enlarged his shop into the Post Office and newsagents. The "Mace" shop was a dairy ran by Mr. and Mrs. R. Harris who left the village during the 1930s.

Rock Hill, 1949

This general view of just one part of the village shows how changes take place quickly and sometimes without people realising the effects. The picture was taken from the churchyard. The White House now stands on the site of Belle View.

Bottom of Fore Street

This pre-war scene shows the lower part of Fore Street well known to the senior citizens of the village. Unfortunately the houses, often very small, were not up to modern day standards, some sharing toilet facilities and a common tap. They were demolished in the 1960s to make way for the present council houses. Carolyn and Valerie Pilgrim and Owen Bryant can be seen in their doorway.

St. Mary's Church Tower

This very fine fifteenth century pinnacled tower forms a prominent landmark in the locality. The present church replaced an earlier one which existed here even before the Norman Conquest of England. It takes its name from the re-dedication in 1318 and has undergone restoration work mainly during the last century. The whole building blends extremely well with the area and contains many interesting memorials and early woodwork.

St. Mary's Church & War Memorial, Tamerton Foliot.

Road, Leading through Village of Tamerton Foliot.

The War Memorial

These two views of the stone memorial shows how this part of the village looked before the Second World War with the narrow main road coming down past the church to the bottom of the village. Tamerton, like many other villages, lost men in the Great War whose names are engraved on the memorial added to which are those of the 1939-45 conflict. The wide footpath in both photographs has gone.

Some Village People

Old Granny Gloyn can be seen above; she was one of the two village nurses and midwives the other being Granny King. Mrs. E. Bereton is holding her niece, Betty Tutton, outside one of Lambert's Cottages. The Bryant family is seen here outside 3 Rock Hill in 1915 with William, Irene, Henry, Arthur, Cyril and Minnie the baby. Another view of the King's Arms, Fore Street, with the former cottages next to it.

Mr. Bill Sobey's Horse and Cart

This photograph will bring back memories of how goods were nearly all delivered years ago. Here Mr. Foxwell (died 1928) is standing next to his horse, on the vegetable round coming up Fore Street. Mr. Sobey later sold produce from his house.

Tamerton Creek

This early view of the creek is looking towards the village on the left of which is Mr. Colwill's house, Salt's Wharf. The tidal waters carried traffic and trade to and from Tamerton but now this is a peaceful and quiet part of the area.

Mr. Foxwell

This full view of the horse and cart was taken outside. Mr. Sobey's house, Kemp's Cottages. This stood next to the chapel, but like many others, it has been demolished. The delivery cart and horse were once a well loved part of the village scene not causing as much noise as today's car.

Mrs. Floyd's Char-a-banc Outing

This early 1920s group was made up of M. Wyatt, E. Collins, Mrs. Wyatt, Mrs. Pederick, Mr. Partridge (driver), A. Pederick, E. Gregory, M. Langman, G. Wyatt, P. Willcocks, M. Pederick, B. Pederick, Mr. Floyd, F. Floyd, D. Pederick, A. Langman, Mrs. Floyd, Mrs. Sobey, Mr. Sobey, G. Floyd, Mrs. Bissett, Mr. Bissett, Gran Smith, J. Smith and D. Sladon besides others.

Mrs. Floyd's Char-a-banc Outing

Another group of outing enthusiasts are seen here including Mrs. Floyd, Mr. Floyd, F. Floyd, E. Floyd, A. Floyd, J. Floyd, Mrs. King, E. King, W. King, Mrs. Tutton, B. Tutton, Mrs. Wyatt, Mrs. Morgan, Lily and Violet Morgan (twins), Mrs. Vickery, Mrs. Pinney and family, Mr. Lake, Mrs. Lake, E. Sobey and W. Sobey.

Village Outings

These were very popular before the widespread use of the car probably reaching their height during the 1930s with the growth of local private bus owners. The village folk took advantage of these new facilities and thought nothing of making long journeys to the moor or coast in open char-a-bancs with solid tyres on the wheels! The middle group shows the ladies of the village during an outing in 1930.

Tamerton Football Team, 1930

This photograph is thought to be that of the team for 1930 and shows S. Hitchcock, W. Blackler, W. Sobey, W. Rounsefull, A. Bryant, J. Floyd, C. Clare, J. Maker, C. Bryant, E. Sobey, J. Kitts, S. Sleep and G. Cave.

Tamerton A.F.C., 1934-35

These were the winners of the Devon League Championship's Amateur Cup. Members are A. Pederick, W. Sobey, L. Maker, A. Swanson, J. Floyd, W. Bryant, W. Gaylard, W. Stevens, T. Morgan, W. Sobey (senior), J. Garlard, B. Smith E. Sobey and others.

Tamerton Football Team in the mid-1930s

Another group of players are seen here from the '30s. Identified among them are C. Maddock, F. Brighton, R. Gray, Les Maker, G. Tilbury, A. Bryant, B. Bryant, T. Brown, B. Stevens, B. Smith, C. Bryant, E. Stevens and E. Sobey. This decade was a very good one for Tamerton when interest in this sport was high and teams had a good following.

A Shire Horse in the Village

This very amusing and touching scene shows Jack Floyd being given a ride on the large shire horse, *Prince,* normally used for ploughing and hauling heavy loads. A definite bygone scene which also shows the state of Fore Street surface; note the bread waggon further down the hill!

Mr. Floyd on his Donkey

This biblical-like scene shows Mr. Floyd on his donkey, not an uncommon way of getting around long before the car came. He worked for Mr. F. Hendy and was the first local person to drive a tractor when they came into the area. It was driven along the then new Station Road to test the surface for normal road traffic.

The Bryant Family, 1923

This family photograph dates from 1923 and was taken on Rock Hill. It shows William and Mary Bryant with their children William, Harry, Arthur, Cyril, Charles, Reginald and Bert with Irene and Minnie, nine members of one Bryant family now the longest living in the village for successive generations.

Memories from 1939-45

The above illustration is dated 1940 and shows girls sorting out picked anemones ready for despatch on the London bound train from Plymouth. Seen here are M. Crocker, Mrs. V. Bryant, M. Rounsefull, V. Rounsefull, H. Crocker and Mrs. E. MacDonald at work. A mixed class of local children and London evacuees from the Willesdon and Acton areas are seen below with Mr. Murray the headmaster, the year was 1940. Raymond Maker, Lenna Medland, Robin Finnemore, Nora Bryant, Charles Sampson and Molly Smith have been identified in the group on an air raid/gas mask drill.

The Vicarage, about 1921
The Mother's Union was well supported in the village; here the cake stall helped local funds at the Vicarage. Mrs. Brighton Mrs. Maker, Mrs. Newcombe and Mrs. Lamble are helping for the day.

Mothers' Union Outing
Tamertonians at Cheddar Caves Somerset! This happy group of villagers and children were well pleased with their journey to the Mendip Hills sometime during the 1930s which was one of many undertaken quite often in open chara-bancs.

Victory Celebrations, 1945
Tamerton rejoiced in the ending of war as enthusiastically as any other village. Here can be seen the Victory Queen's Float with Nora Bryant as Queen. In attendance are Margaret Gaylard, Francis Chanter, Jill Pilgrim, Carol Lesley, Christine Smith, Keith Langman and Mrs. Maddock (senior) who crowned the Queen.

Mary Dean's School, 1921

Back row: J. Floyd, J. Gaylard, R. Maddock, M. Cann. *First row:* Mr. Lucas, schoolmaster, P. Pedrick, W. Osborne, W. Sobey, C. Cave, W. Blackler, J. Horton, A. Caunter, P. Langford, J. Leyman. *Sitting:* E. Sleep, M. Robinson, M. Vicary, B. Chanter, R. Gillard, B. Gillard, L. Olver, M. King, M. Gregory. *Front row:* E. Sobey, S. Sleep, W. Blackmore, F. Summers, L. Maker, F. Lavers, S. Northnore and C. Deacon.

A Proud Bride

Ethel Morgan is seen here proudly wearing the wedding gown in which she had been married in 1911. The group are in the garden of Belle View and show Aunt Bess Morgan with three of her daughters Bessie, Hettie and Ethel.

The Chapel Garden, 1929

Posed against this well decorated fruit and flower stall as part of the annual event have been recognised Mrs. Sleeman, Mrs. Hoskin, Mrs. Clapham, Kitty Maddock and B. Northaway. The enthusiasm for these kinds of occasions still continue in the village today.

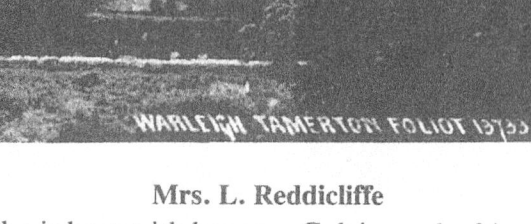

Warleigh Dovecote
This unique local building was erected in 1600 with 500 nest holes standing close to Warleigh Manor. Doves and other birds were a source of fresh meat during the winter months years ago.

Warleigh Manor
This postcard view of the manor house of about 50 years ago shows all the front of the building and the different levels of the garden. From 1741 to 1970 it was the home of the Radcliffe family, the local squires, one of whom had it remodelled to the designs of John Foulston. It is now a modern nursing home.

Mrs. L. Reddicliffe
She is here with her son, Galvin, and a friend outside her cottage in Fore Street in the 1920s. She and her husband were caretakers of the village hut; she was a good organiser of dances, jumble sales, etc. known for her dressing up as well as playing the concertina. She also organised the Benevolent Fund for returning servicemen after 1945.

Slaughter House Pump
Sited above a spring this pump was used for many years for cleaning purposes in the village slaughter house. It was last used during the war for supplying drinking water when the normal supplies had been damaged.

Cann House, a Cheshire Home

This recent view of Cann House shows to good effect this large Victorian mansion built in 1863 and now well known in the area as a Cheshire Home for the disabled. It was given by the last family to live here, the Tucketts, and has been used for the disabled since 1959.

Cann House Fetes

Garden fetes and bazaars have long been very popular at Cann House. The two large photographs show part of the 1930 fete with K. Newcombe, Mrs. Newcombe, Mrs. Millman, Mrs. Uxman, Mrs. Brighton, E. Bereton, Mrs. Brock and B. Tutton, Mrs. Floyd is the elderly lady with the windmill. Mrs. D. Grigg of Cann House is in the above photograph.

Fore Street between the Wars

A view that has considerably changed as all the cottages on the right have gone! Mr. Bill Kendall can be seen at the door of his cobblers shop just above the Old Post Office. The island shop still stands as do the buildings on the left.

Fore Street

This inter-war photograph shows the old Post Office on the left with the mail van parked outside it while on the right the tall building with the steps was the old Tamar House Hotel, once a coaching inn. This view has altered considerably with the demolition of the houses on the left. Miss Lilian Dingle was the postmistress.

Lower end of Fore Street

This view probably dates from 1921. Mary Jane Luscombe, an old village "character", used to live in one of the cottages long demolished with those shown here. Floods frequently covered the lower part of the road sometimes isolating her and neighbours in their homes when the village boys would row in milk and other daily supplies. The tree marks the entrance path to the old parish hall. A later flooding caused the high wall to collapse.

Cross roads at top of Fore Street

Mrs. Win Dulling can be seen here standing outside her cottage just above the Methodist Chapel. Memories fade with time but this one recalls many houses facing Fore Street which are now gone including hers. The houses made up a compact area.

The Village Blacksmith

This view of Star Lane is looking towards Fore Street. The double black doors on the left was where the blacksmith worked; the buildings are now demolished. Mr. Ambrose Octavius Facey, to give him his full name, was a very jolly figure and is well remembered by many children as he allowed them to watch him at work. The forge later became a garage repair shop.

St. Mary's Church

This well balanced view of the village church was probably taken early in the morning as it shows some mist in the valley. The photograph could have been taken from the fields below Drunken Lane. It dates from the 1930s.

Village Milestone

This granite milestone gives distances from Tamerton to Tavistock, Plymouth and Dock (Devonport)

1935 Coronation and Digging for Victory

Time for a teabreak during the village celebrations for the 1935 Coronation held in Cann House field, J. Floyd is in the middle playing the drum, H. Chanter with the melodion and others looking on are Mrs. E. Vicary, Mrs. Osborne, Mrs. M. Bryant, B. Bryant, C. Gray and H. Bryant. Farming at Warleigh Barton during the last war using horses because of petrol shortages. Ron Stevenson and Jim Mills are playing their part in making the country self sufficient in food.

Electricity comes to Tamerton

This most unusual photograph shows Dick Floyd in charge of the electric generator, switch board and battery room at Mr. Hendys in 1925. Mr. Floyd was also one of the dairy farm hands working at *Cressy* where Mr. Hendy introduced electricity to the village farm then later to the chapel across the road and then to the village itself. This fine piece of pioneering work was well ahead of the years when the main supply reached Tamerton from Plymouth. Tamerton railway bridge was always in need of some kind of maintenance or other. Here a group of men under the guidance of Captain Kitts, with pipe in mouth, pose against the background of the bridge's girders. He was also paid to guide local steamers under it as a good knowledge of the changing tides and currents was necessary to ensure a safe passage.

The Chapel awaits the Guest of Honour

The above picture is thought to be a welcoming party for the guest of honour to open the fruit or harvest banquet at the chapel. The scene is from 1923 and present are M. Lamble, F. Hitchcock, A. Wyatt, I. Olver, L. Olver, L. and V. Morgan (twins), D. Chanter, B. Chanter, V. Rounsefull, M. Bryant, W. Sobey, J. Floyd, M. Millman, A. Floyd, E. Floyd, Mr. and Mrs. Sobey, Mr. Hendy and the Pedrick boys. 1930/31 is the season for Tamerton A.F.C. seen below with W. Morgan, W. Bryant, G. Tilbury, L. Maker, A. Bryant, J. Floyd, J. Brighton, C. Maddock, H. Bryant, W. Stevens, J. Gaylard, W. Smith, W. Sobey and sitting is T. Brown and E. Sobey.

Mr. Pilgrim's First Shop
Like many servicemen after the Second World War, L. J. Pilgrim started his own business after being demobbed. W. Kendall is standing in his first shop and he later took on the grocery, newsagent and Post Office shop in the Fore Street. Below is the late Bill Kendall standing in his own boot and shoe repair shop doorway. This building has also been demolished.

Mrs. Vicary's Shop
Old Mrs. Vicary is here seen standing in the door of her shop and her daughter, Mrs. B. Rickard, looking down from the first floor window. It was part of Stoke Cottages in the Fore Street. Mrs. Rickard later took over the shop followed by Mr. Pilgrim, the last shopkeeper before the building was demolished.

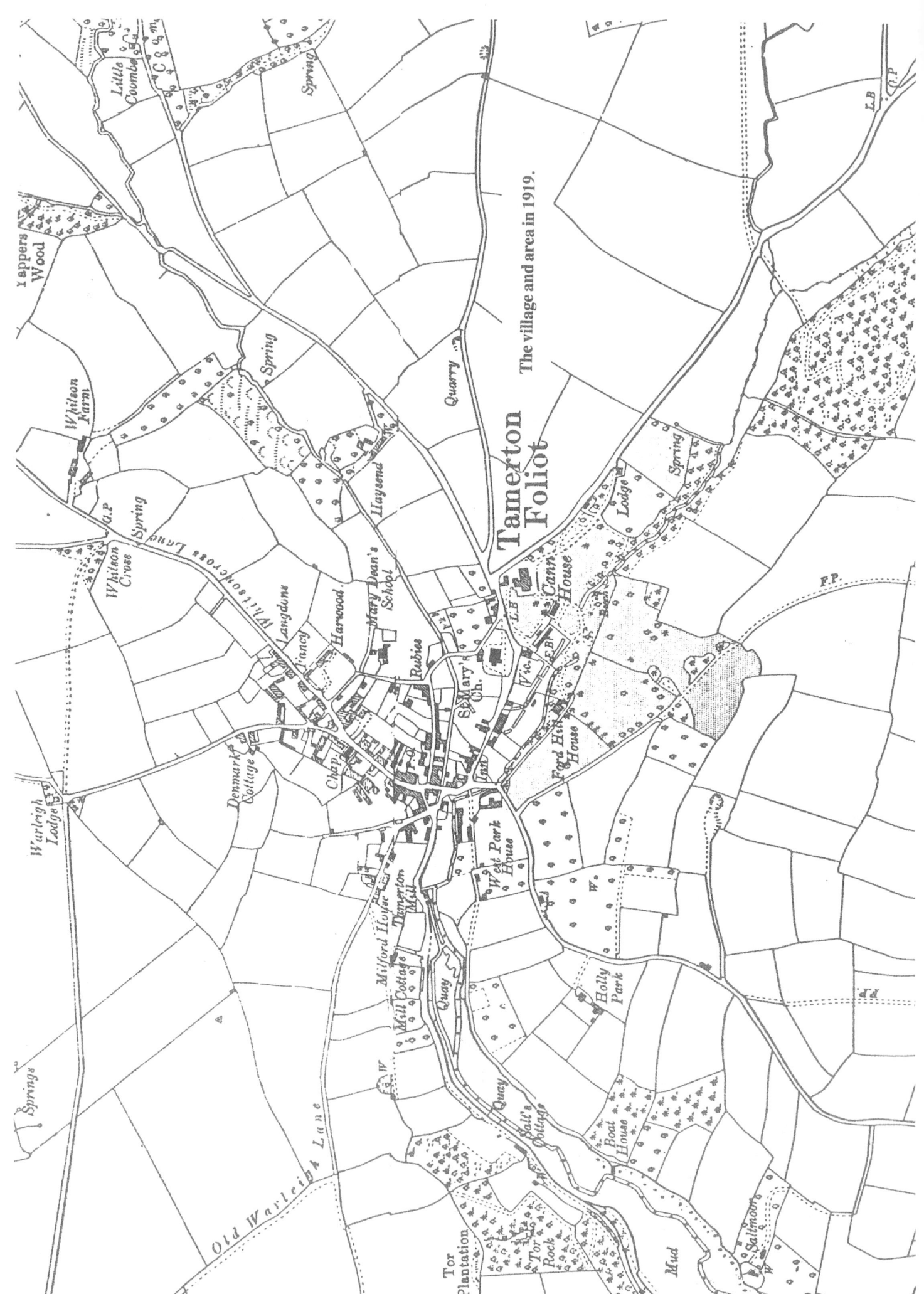

Tamerton Foliott.

Is a village and parish situated at the confluence of the Tamar and Tavy rivers, five miles N.W. from Plymouth, in the south-east or Tavistock division of the county, Roborough hundred, and county court district of Stonehouse. The Church of St Mary was built in 1818, in the reign of Edward the Second. A memorial clock, with chimes striking the quarters and hours, has been placed in the tower in remembrance of Mark E. Grigg, Esq., is in the Perpendicular style with a handsome square, embattled tower, containing a peal of six bells. In the interior are monuments to members of the Copleston, Bamfhylde, and Radcliffe families; a stained window was placed in 1887, in memory of General Macan. The north aisle has been rebuilt from plans by Mr. Fellowes Prynne. The living is a vicarage, in the gift of the Lord Chancellor. There is a parochial endowed school founded 1734 for boys and girls. About £50 is annually distributed among the poor from the Maristow Charity and the gifts of various benevolent individuals. Maristow, the seat of Right Hon. Sir Massey Lopes, Bart., is in this parish. The ancient manor-house, situated at Warleigh, on the banks of the Tavy, about a mile from the village is the property of Walter Radcliffe, Esq., the lord of the manor. The population in 1881, was 1,147, and in 1891, 1,118. The South Western Railway passes through Warleigh Wood where a station has been built.

POST, TELEGRAPH, SAVINGS BANK and MONEY ORDER OFFICE,—Fredk. Dingle, postmaster. Letters received 7.5 a.m. 2.10 p.m. and 4.20 p.m., and despatch'd 9.30, 12.10 p.m., 6.30 p.m. weekdays, and 9.5 a.m., Sundays, via Plymouth. Wall letter box opposite Church cleared 9.10, 12.15 a.m. and 6.35 p.m.; Sundays 9.35 a.m. Wall box bottom Looseleigh lane, 9.25 a.m.; 12.30 and 6-50 p.m. Sundays, 9.50 a.m.

CHURCH (St. Mary)—Rev. Edward Roberts, M.A. vicar
CHAPEL—Wesleyan
CONVALESCENT HOME,—Chairman, R. Reynolds Fox; matron, Miss Phear.
ASSISTANT OVERSEER—Henry Huxham
PAROCHIAL SCHOOL—Walter Brown, master; Mrs W. Brown, mistress
PARISH COUNCIL—Clerk, Henry Huxham
RAILWAY STATION.—Warleigh Wood, Robert Caseley, station master

PRIVATE RESIDENTS. 1900

Bayley Capt. Jno. Heathfield
Briggs Miss, Down house
Bulteel Jas. C. M.B. Looseleigh
Fox Francis J.P., Uplands
Fox Richard Reynolds, Westbrook
Fox Walter R. 4 Delgany villas
Grigg Henry, Cann house
Jackman William, the Berry
James Jno. B, Tamerton house
Julian Miss, Oakfield
Julian Mrs Francis, Southdown lawn
Keats W, Osborn, 2 Delgany villas
Lander Joseph, Langdons
Lister Edward Wm, Little Powisland
Luke Mrs Alice, 3 Delgany villas
Northcott Richard, Wadlands house
Pillar Edward, Ford hill
Prowse George, Mount View
Ralph Admiral, West Park house
Richardson Miss Harret, Brookfield
Guile Capt., A.B.A., Greenbank
Roberts Rev Edward M.A. (vicar) The Vicarage
Salmon Miss Emma, 2 Prospect villas
Walford Col. R.A. Warleigh
Winnicott Captain Samuel R.N, 1 Prospect vls
Woodley John L. C. 1 Delgany villas

COMMERCIAL.

Arthur John Jonathan, farmer, Horsham
Avery George, farmer, Clittaford
Ball Samuel, farmer, Langley farm
Bassett John, farmer, Webber's farm
Bawden Samuel, carpenter
Bickle Henry, wheelwright
Brown Walter, schoolmaster
Callaway Wm. market gardener, Hillside
Cazeley Robert, station master
Cole John, farmer, Haysend
Cole Jno. Edwin, farmer, Dunsbeer
Collins James, market gardener
Collins James, tailor
Dennis John, farmer, Broadleigh farm
Dingle Fredk, bootmaker and postmaster
Ellacott John farmer, Coombe farm
Ellis James, market gardener
Ellis John, farmer, Henwell farm
Fenlon N, agent for Sir Massey Lopes, Bart.
Finnemore Wm. market gardener and King's Arms
German John, farmer, Broadley
Gillard John, farmer, Coombe farm
Gillard Wm. market gardener, Allern
Gregory Albert, market gardener
Gregory Mrs Caroline, Queen's Arms
Gregory Matthew, market gardener, Rock hill house
Hacker Mrs, farmer, Birdcage
Hacker Joseph, farmer, Trehills farm
Hamand Henry, George hotel
Hamley R. farmer, Blaxton
Harris Arthur Henry, tailor
Harris Herbert, shoemaker
Harvey Richard, market gardener
Hendy John, market gardener and dairyman
Hendy Jno. jun. market gardener
Hill Thos. farmer, Bulteel's Bickham
Hoskins Richd. dairyman and market gardener
Huxham Hy. dairyman & assistant overseer
Irish Richard, Seven Stars
Knight Miss, general shop
Leeman John, dairyman
Lovell Wm. farmer, Pound farm
Luke Wm, farmer, Poorsham farm
Luscombe Mrs F. G. farmer, Warleigh Barton
Maddock Andrew, carpenter, etc
Maddock Emanuel, farmer, Charity Bickham
Maddock George, carpenter and undertaker
Maddock John, farmer, Southway farm
March James, yeoman, Widewell farm
Mason James, market gardener, Torr
Millman Samuel, mason and shopkeeper
Nicholls Ed, J, farmer, Ashleigh
Northcott John, mason, Rosedews
Northcott Richard, builder, Wadlands house
Packer, Henry & George, market gardeners
Pengelly Wm. Hy. farmer, Whitson farm
Pethick John, wheelwright and miller
Redding John, mason
Rational Sick and Burial Society (Wm. Trout, branch sec), meetings are held at King's arms 2nd Saturday in each month
Stancombe R. Henshire's farm
Tamerton Horticultural Society (Hy. Huxham, hon tres, Callaway A., Loveday G. hon secs.)
Tamar Arms Temperance Refreshment house (Fredk. Dingle)
Trout W. G. blacksmith
Vanstone William, farmer, Broadley
Veal William, coal merchant
Vicary Charles, carrier and shopkeeper
Williams Edwin, shopkeeper and baker
Woodley James, butcher
Wyatt F. T. plumber

Lists of Local People

During the past 100 years lists of local businesses and people have been produced from time to time giving details of who was working, private residents and other details. Three years are shown here for Tamerton which now make interesting reading.

TAMERTON FOLIOTT.
PRIVATE RESIDENTS.

Bawden Edward, gardener
Bawden Richard, carpenter
Brewer Thomas, schoolmaster
Briggs William
Brooking James
Brown James, rate collector
Calloway William, smith
Chaffe Henry
Dunn John, shopkeeper
Ellis John   1878
Ewing Miss Emily
Fitz Miss Jane
Goulding Frank H., goldsmith, Tamerton house
Grigg Mrs. Catherine, postmistress
Grigg M., Cann cottage
Grigg William, Heathfield house
Hawken Charles
Jeffrey John
King's Arms Inn, Richard Northcott
Liscombe R. L, Uplands
Luke Frederick J., baker, &c.
Maddock George, carpenter
Mason John, wood dealer
Maynard Edward
Northcott John, mason
Packer George, mason, &c.
Pearse Miss Agnes
Pearse Mrs. Eliza, shopkeeper
Penwarden J., beer retailer
Pepperell Ann, beer retailer
Prideaux O., Westbrook
Queen's Arms, Matthew H. Gregory
Radcliffe Rev. W. J. P., Warleigh
Rickard James, tailor
Roberts Rev. Edwin, vicarage
Smith Samuel
Stephens John, carpenter
Stoyle Samuel, shopkeeper
Toms William, gardener

TAMERTON FOLIOTT.
PRIVATE RESIDENTS.

Arthur Rev. George, Vicarage
Baron Mr. John
Batten Mrs.
Briggs William, Esq.   1867
Brown Mrs. Broadley
Grigg M. Esq. Cann Cottage
Grigg Mr. Williams, Heathfield House
Lopes Sir Massey, Bart. J.P. Maristow
Luscombe R. Esq. Uplands
Munroe Capt. Roborough House
Prideaux C. Esq. Westbrook
Radcliffe Rev. W. J.P. Warleigh
Smith Miss, Alwyn View

COMMERCIAL.

Arthur J. farmer, Horsham
Bawden Richard, carpenter
Blackmore William, shoemaker
Callaway William, smith
Dunn James, shopkeeper
Gloyn John, carpenter
Gregory M. Queen's Arms
Hacker John, farmer, Birdcage
Harris George, butcher
Helson George, King's Arms
Jack Albert, surgeon
Kingwell James, George Hotel
Lillicrap John, butcher
Maddock John, carpenter
March John, auctioneer, &c.
Northcott J. & R. masons
Pearce J. shoemaker
Pearse P.   ditto
Pepperell J. beer retailer
Roberts Mrs. Nursery
Smith Mrs. grocer
Stoyle S. shopkeeper and druggist
Wade —, collector of taxes

Mary Dean's School, 1922

Among those recognised in this group are Violet and Lily Morgan (twins), Betty Tutton, Mary Stevens, Ester Collins, Dorothy Clements, Minnie Bryant, Ruth Gloyn, Elsie King, Eppie Floyd, William Stevens. Dolly Kendal, Bob Bereton and George Kitts. The photograph was taken in the school playground.

Mary Dean's School, 1910

This earlier group shows J. Finnemore, C. Daniel, G. Olver, J. Pearce, S. Hunt, D. Harvey, B. Collins, B. Lamble, T. Smith, M. Leyman, G. Penna, P. Floyd, A. Penna, and A. Bickle. The teacher is Miss Marian Calloway. Seated on stools are F. Hitchcock, H. Cole, L. Floyd, E. Sleep and, on the ground, W. Bryant. There are also others in the group.

Mary Dean's School, 1922

Yet another group from the old village school who include R. Bryant, C. Bryant, C. Bryant, B. Bryant F. Stevens, Daisy Sladden and the school mistress Mrs. Hocking.

Mary Dean's Church School, 1734-1976

The school name commemorates an endowment given by Mary Dean of Marystow in 1734 for providing education for originally twenty poor boys living within the parish. Many generations of pupils have benefited through the school two groups of which are seen on this page. The above shows the school netball team of 1924, Ruth Gloyn, Minnie Bryant, Mary Steven, Elsie King, Lily and Violet Morgan and the one below, taken in 1940, shows the headmaster, Mr. Hooper, and others recognised as Graham Bibbings, Robin Finnemore, Leonard Morgan, Peirce Stevents, Muriel MacDonald, Nora Bryant, Francis Chanter, Mary Gaylard, Mary Langman, Christine Stephenson and, in the front row, Molly Smith, Lena Medland, Betty Bellamy and Kathleen Horswell.

Strawberry Feast

This photograph was taken in the late 1930s and shows a group enjoying a rest during one of the annual feasts. The people have not been recognised, apart from the lady standing Mrs. Eppie Floyd and Roy Maddock, but maybe a reader will spot who the others are. This event has always been a popular one in the local calendar.

Strawberry Feast

An earlier photograph thought to be from about 1930 shows yet again local people enjoying refreshments at the feast or fair. The fair remains but the styles of clothing and hats change to such an extent that the period can be easily identified.

Fore Street

The narrow street with overhanging trees and foliage in front of the Methodist Chapel contrasts with the same scene today. The street is broader and, of course, many of the houses are gone. The chapel is the home of the famous "Tamerton Strawberry Feast or Fair".

Dairymen of the Village

This group was taken in 1926 and among those recognised are G. Pederick, H. Lamble and Mr. Linder. No doubt others will be identified. It shows Mr. Hendy and some of his men and lads. The right hand building is *Cressy;* others are Almshouses, the Wardens House which fronted onto Lodge Hill. It housed the village lock up cell in its basement!

First Council Houses

This working party was nearing the completion of the first council houses to be built in the village. It was taken 1928-29 at Harwood Villas, now Whitsoncross Lane. Most of those here are from Plympton but some locals are included. W. Bryant, Mrs. A. Wyatt, Mr. Bridgeman, C. May and Mr. Wyatt. The building contractor was also from Plympton.

1923 Tree Planting Ceremony

This group was photographed after the ceremony at Mr. Hendy's of *Cressy* following the old tree being blown down. In it are Mr. Linder, Mr. Hendy, G. Petherick, B. Chanter, Mrs. Dymond, C. Chanter, E Floyd, Mrs. Floyd, Mrs. Reddicliffe, W. Morgan, C. Morgan, D. Clements, J. Leyman, L. Pengelly and Mrs. Hancock.

The 1947 Carnival and Queen

All the joy of the occasion is captured by the smiles on the Queen's and her attendants' faces as they arrive for the 1947 village carnival watched by children in Harwood Avenue. The Queen is Beryl Southwood and her attendants are Pauline Rounsefull, Mary Gregory, Cynthia Cummings and Little Miss Courtier. St. Mary's Church is in the background and the bell and tower of the old Mary Dean's School. Below is the carnival in full spate with many children in fancy dress followed by supporting villagers.

Mrs. Finnemore's Old Time Dancing evenings, about 1948

This large group of local people amply show the enthusiasm for these events especially following the last war. Seen here is Mrs. Finnemore, Jill Pilgrim, Norren Sobey, Marjory Cann, Brian Rounsefull, Hazel Wadling, Terry and David Finnemore, Mrs. Rounsefull, Dinah Smith, Phylis Wildman, Mrs. Turpin, Mrs. Harvey, Mrs. Cordell, Mrs. Lampshire, Mrs. Mead, Mrs. Chanter, Joan Damerell, B. Collick, Mrs. Burford, Mrs. Dymond, Mrs. Wyatt, Joyce Maker, Mrs. Paul, Mrs. Reddicliffe and many others. The 1945 Victory Queen, Nora Bryant and attendants on their float with Rear-Admiral and Mrs. Hosking and Mrs. Clapham in the foreground. Ronald Northey, Tony Smith and Joan Wildman are recognised as the children to the right of the float.

The Coplestone Oak Tree

Sited on the remains of the village green this very old oak tree takes its name from Christopher Coplestone, one time Lord of the Manor. He is reputed to have stabbed his godson to death here. Note the young person hiding in the hollow trunk.

D.M.T. Buses - the First

These two pictures are of the first regular bus service to the village from Plymouth by the Devon Motor Transport company. The driver was W. Ellicott and the conductor M. Lamble, also a villager. The bus was garaged overnight in old Warleigh Lane so it would be ready for the next morning's 6.20 a.m. Dockyard run. The photographs date from the 1920s.

Star Lane
An old part of the village long gone and lastly used to house war-time evacuees during the 1939-45 war. The Queen's Arms inn is on the right seen from the Fore Street end. The Publican was Jim Paul.

Station Road
This sylvan scene is at the second hill along Station Road with Mr. Bert Paddon pushing his bicycle up it. His parents owned the island shop for many years and he, being later crippled, would sit behind the counter all day selling sweets and cigarettes.

Bampfylde Almshouses
This copy of an early print shows Mrs. Cordell in the yard of Bampfylde Almshouses which were erected in 1827 for poor people. Latterly they were used for housing people waiting for council accommodation. Mrs. Cordell came to the village from London with her husband and she is still living in Tamerton.

Fancy Dress Ball and Children Singing

One of the many fancy dress evenings organised by Mr.Frederick Hancock (standing far right in upper picture dressed as a minstrel) held in the parish hut during 1928. Among the revellers are Mrs. Reddicliffe and Bill, Mrs. Smith, Winnie Vickers, Minnie Bryant, Eileen Stevens, the Morgan twins, and Mrs. Jones and Francis who ran the fish and chip shop. Below is a 1938 group of Sunday School scholars who gave the traditional Wednesday evening presentation of hymns and songs following the annual anniversary. Catherine Finnemore, Eva and Margo Howard, Billy Bryant, David Tozer, Robin Finnemore, Raymond Maker, Raymond and Pauline Rounsefull, Charlie Sampson, Betty and Mary Bellamy, Mary Gaylard, Mary Langman and Nora Bryant can be seen.

Arthur L. Clamp – the man behind the books

Arthur Leslie Clamp was a man of boundless energy with a passion for helping others, particularly through his love of history. A printer by trade, he started his career in a printing company before moving his family from Exeter to Plymouth to teach at the Plymouth College of Art and Design, where he eventually became the Head of the Printing Department.

Arthur with his five children.

A Devoted Family Man

Despite his love of teaching, Arthur prioritised his family, always making it home by 5:30pm for tea. He and his wife, Rosemary, raised five children: Susan, Angela, Elizabeth, David, and Steven. Arthur would often combine his love of family and history by taking his children on Sunday walks, encouraging them to appreciate historical monuments by taking photos or making crayon rubbings of gravestones for his books. The family home at 203 Elburton Road was a hub of activity, with a large garden, featuring a two-storey fort and a makeshift swimming pool.

A Lifelong Learner and Adventurer

Arthur's thirst for knowledge extended beyond history to a deep curiosity about the world. He was passionate about exploring different cultures, traditions, and cuisines, often taking advantage of his long summer holidays as a teacher to travel to places like India, Russia, South America, the middle east and the USA, sometimes bringing one of his children along. This adventurous spirit even influenced his home life, as seen by the short-lived family tradition of steam-cooking vegetables after a trip to Iceland.

History is a prominent feature of family days out

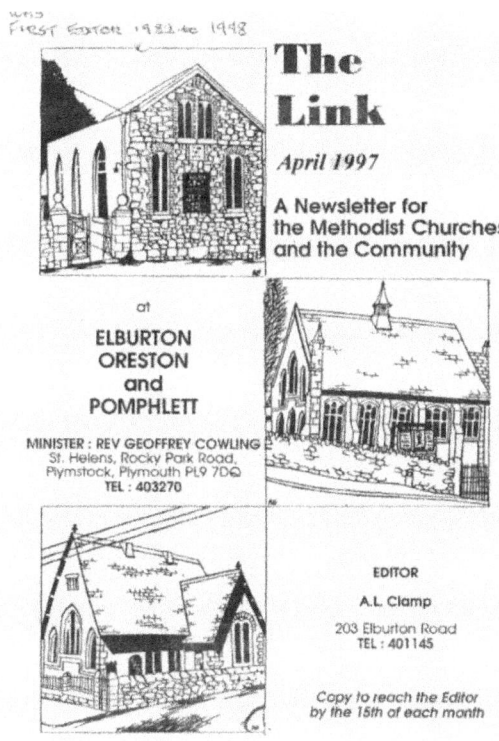

Community and Philanthropic Spirit

His commitment to serving others was evident in his long-standing involvement with the Elburton Methodist Church. He was the Sunday School Superintendent for over 15 years and served as the editor of the wider church's monthly newsletter, "The Link," for a similar duration. After Rosemary's very sad passing, Arthur later remarried and, following a chance encounter with a professor from India, established a connection with a missionary school in Chennai. Together with his new wife, Christine, he co-founded a "Sponsor a Child's Education" program that continues to this day.

*Pictured left – The cover of 'The Link' complete
with hand drawn sketches of each church by Angela
Below right – Arthur Clamp promoting his latest book
Below left – Arthur at home with his first wife, Rosemary
Below centre – Arthur on holiday with his second wife,
Christine*

A Legacy of Learning and Positivity

Arthur's greatest passion was history, which he brought to life through tireless research, documentation, and the many books he authored. He was driven by a need to "never be stuck in a rut," constantly seeking new experiences, meeting new people, and expanding his knowledge. With a positive attitude and a great sense of humour, he was always ready to help others, leaving a lasting impact on his family and community. His children, Susan, Angela, Elizabeth, David, and Steven, remember him with love and gratitude.

David Clamp, 2025

A Legacy of Local History

Below is the story of how Arthur L Clamp began writing books, in his own words, drafted shortly before he passed away in 2001. I have only made minor alterations to this text, correcting grammatical errors that he did not survive to correct himself. When I first discovered this text, I was shocked to see my name mentioned. It seems that, unbeknownst to me, I shared my first PC with him. I suspect he used it during the day when I was at school, although I do have one memory of sitting with him and showing him how it worked. It has been a pleasure to pick up where he left off and see his books republished and redistributed, and to know that I was part of the story, even back then. It was also fascinating to discover that his pricing structure matches the way I have tried to price the books, with a third going to local sellers and the rest covering printing costs with a little left over for my expenses.

I am his eldest grandson, and it is a privilege to curate his legacy, which we are calling 'The Clamp Collection'. The very last line of the text originally reads "The following pages list all the titles." Sadly, that page is missing and we have no record of all the books he published and knowing that some of those were researched by other authors makes the process of finding them even harder. I look forward to one day completing the collection and seeing them all available again. And maybe, one day, I'll even start writing my own to add to the series. For now, here is his story in his own words.

Steven Gibson, 2025

Writing and Publishing Booklets on Local Topics and Areas

I started this interest in either 1968 or 1969 when living in Woodford. I had by these dates established the Department of Printing and I think I must have been looking for something different to do. The first titles were of A5 size proofed from type set at Clarke, Doble and Brendon, Ltd., Plymouth printers, and then made up into pages and printed at Sawtell and Neilson, Ltd., Totnes.

Then began a slow process of getting them out to shops, etc. which proved to be more time consuming and difficult than actually researching, writing and getting the books into print. However, I persisted and opened a business account with Barclays Bank on the Broadway. I was advised to give it a title so I called it "Westway Publications". There came along another problem, one of storage of paper and finished books which was solved when the family moved to Elburton in 1970.

I changed the printer to Penwell, Ltd., Callington, Cornwall, as he was then just setting up himself and his prices seemed very reasonable. I did not get any of the printers to make up the complete books. I hand folded the flat printed sheets, stitched the books on a small manual table stitcher and trimmed them in a small hand turned guillotine which I bought from someone in Penzance for £40. It was brought up in a van.

The trouble and time going to and fro to Callington was too much so I transferred the printing to PDS Printers, Prince Rock, Plymouth, and I have been with them ever since. Now they are at Plympton which is easy to reach and they fold the flat sheets which was turning out to be a long chore which only saved a small part of the printing costs.

All my first titles were written by myself. I took the photographs and developed them in the loft of the house, the type was set by now on a computer situated in the house at Elburton from which I had collected photographic lengths of text to cut up and law down as pages.

At some point I decided that I would do my own film processing of lith film so I bought a large second hand process camera from Kingsbridge and learnt through trial and error to make line negatives of the text and halftone negatives of the illustrations which proved more difficult than I anticipated. The main problem was trying to keep the developer in the large dish at the correct temperature as any change would affect the developing time. I replaced this old camera with a brand new one bought from Croydon, Surrey, costing £900. This has turned out to be a great asset cutting out an expensive part of the printer's costs and one crucial aspect of the work which I could control.

By the middle 1970s there were many outlets I had contacted in Plymouth, up to Dartmoor, Exeter, around to Torbay, Totnes, Dartmouth and the South Hams. The market for local books was much greater than I had first thought and through getting to know many local people undertaking research themselves had the chance to help and make up books for other people who had in most instances, got together a collection of photographs with some text in a rather muddled way. Through my experience in print I was able to shape up their work and get it into print and in every case I had to pay the printer and let the person have the royalties. In the majority of titles produced in this manner this was another way of producing titles and it did give some profit to my work. However, I must say that in a few cases I lost out by either the other person getting the numbers wrong, not returning any monies from stock I delivered or they thought that more of their books should have been sold.

The print run was usually 1,000 copies and from time to time I have had reprints of 250 copies. It took about ten years to clear the first print run so I always had large stocks in the garage, workshop, etc. The numbers sold during the early years was about 7,000 copies a year increasing to around 9,000 copies and for the whole of the enterprise about 500,000 have been sold. The booklets have become part of the local scene and many people collect them, shops regularly order copies and I go around certain areas month by month restocking or replacing titles as necessary.

During the past year or so I have started setting the text on a Packard Bell PC, something which I should have done some years back. I share it with Steven Gibson, my grandson. There appears to be no end to the market for local books, but I could not earn a regular income because of the long time it takes to sell stock.

However, now exceeding 100 titles made up mainly of A4 twenty-four page booklets, some folded guides, with selling prices set with a third going to the shop which is the trade custom, the original idea has been quite successful and could go on for ever.

Apart from monetary benefits, however spasmodically these might be, I have learnt a lot myself, met many interesting people and have become part of the local scene with requests to give talks and to advise people about getting into print.

Arthur L Clamp, 2001

Death of local historical author

'He was an incredible character who was just loved by everybody who knew him'

A WELL-loved Elburton author has died at the age of 68.

Arthur Clamp (pictured right), who was one of the West Country's most successful writers, died at St Luke's Hospice, Turnchapel, after losing his battle against cancer.

Tributes have been flooding in for a man who was known in the community as a prominent writer and outgoing person.

He produced more than 140 titles during his life, dealing with both fiction, fact and history, often discussing West Country topics that were close to his heart.

One of his most acclaimed books was *The Plymouth Blitz*, and he also won credit for *The Rise and Fall of the Bearings of Membland Hall*, set in Noss Mayo.

He achieved sales of between 7,000 and 9,000 books every year and it is estimated that he has sold over half a million books, covering the areas of Plymouth, Dartmoor, Exeter, Torbay and the South Hams.

Mr Clamp was born in Mitcham, Surrey, in 1932, and was the eldest of four children.

He moved to Devon in 1941 to avoid the London air-raids.

Mr Clamp trained as a printer in Exeter and also gained a teachers' certificate in 1959 from Garnet College in London.

Plymouth College of Art, however, was to prove to be Mr Clamp's working home for the following 32 years until 1991, when he retired as head of the printing department.

He had a great interest in travel and had visited the USA, Tanzania, China, Russia, Peru, as well as travelling across Europe, where he presented talks and slide shows on his experiences as a writer.

Mr Clamp was a member of Elburton Methodist Church for many years, superintendent of the Sunday school and editor of the church newsletter, as well as being involved in much charity work.

He was president of the Plymouth and District Field Club and an active member of the Elburton Residents' Association.

He enjoyed leading walks on Dartmoor and historical tours throughout the West Country.

Mr Clamp married his first wife, Rosemary, in 1956 and they had five children – Susan, Angela, Elizabeth, David and Steven – and she died in 1987. He also had 11 grandchildren.

He leaves a wife Christine, after remarrying in 1991, and her two children and three grandchildren.

'He was an incredible character who was just loved by everybody who knew him,' said his wife.

'He will be missed by his family, his friends, the people he worked with and just everybody who knew him through his books.'

More than 300 mourners attended his funeral at Elburton Methodist Church on Monday.

'The attendance was a celebration of his life – he would have found that really special. It shows his vibrancy and love of people,' said Mrs Clamp.

Steven Clamp added that his father was 'a well respected and loved man, missed by a great many people throughout the South West and far beyond'.

This newspaper article, published by the Evening Herald on 17th August 2001, forms a good record of his life. Just as he encourages us to learn more about local history, we encourage you to learn a little about him. For that reason, we have included these pages at the back of all the most recently republished books, in honour of his memory and recognition of his contribution to the community.